MW00527999

Fifty Shades of Pink

S R COOPER

Illustrated by Christie Matis

Copyright © 2014
S R Cooper

All rights reserved.

This book or any portion thereof may not be
reproduced or used in any manner whatsoever
without the express written permission of the publisher
except for the use of brief quotations in a book review.

ISBN: 0-9898803-9-7
ISBN-13: 978-0-9898803-9-8

For Bella & Quinci,
my 100 Shades of Pink,
and Matt,
the True Love who
brought them to me.

With love and gratitude.

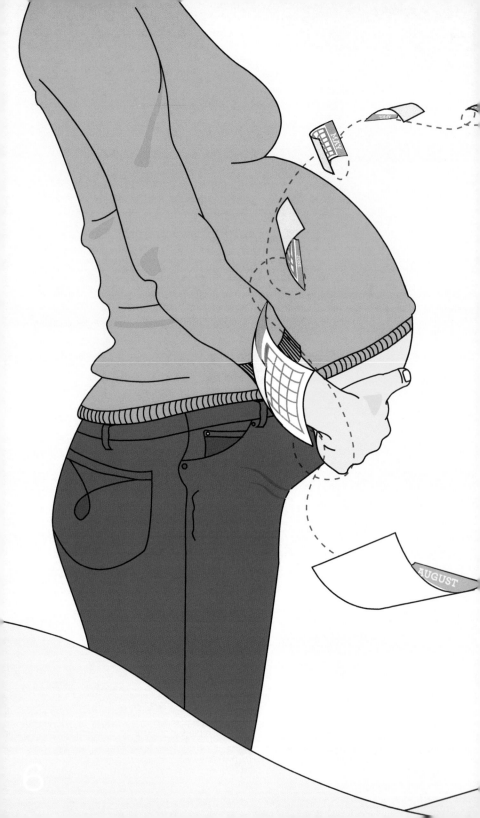

They say
there's been a sudden
baby boom
since 2013,

Nine months or so after
the Fifty Shades series
hit the scene.

This phenomenon dubbed
"mommy porn"
made its way
(to the delight of
these new dads)

To carpool lanes
across the land
on Kindles and iPads.

9

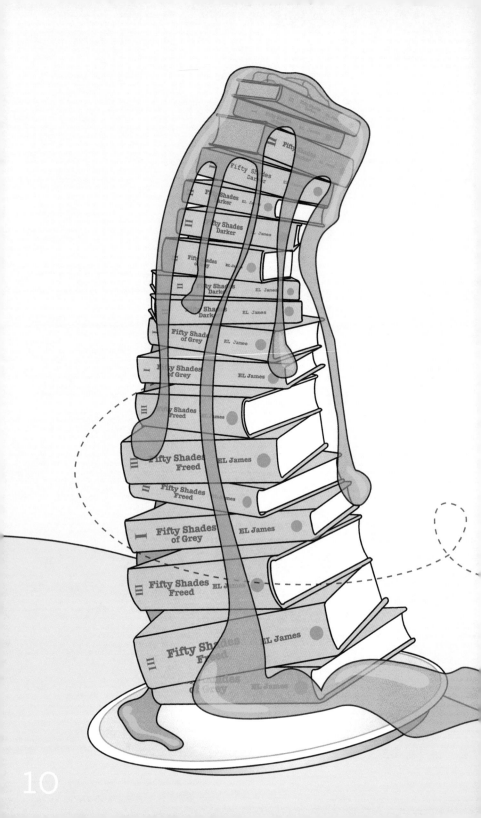

The books all sold
like hot cakes
and were passed
from friend to friend.

A woman's ultimate
fantasy:
he feeds you,
spoils you,
and you can change him
in the end.

11

He shows her
many things
that she never could
dream of.

She surrenders
all control
to end up
with true love.

12

Now all of you
new mommies
are in for a surprise.

The gooey sleeps
you enjoyed last year
will be the last ones
of your lives.

WAAAAAAAAAAAAAAA!

15

It is YOU
who will be doing
all the feeding,
spoiling
and changing.

There's no way
you could have known,
now lives and souls
need rearranging.

You will be overtaken
by this little being
without abatement.

You'll get "More" and
TRUE LOVE is, at best,
an understatement.

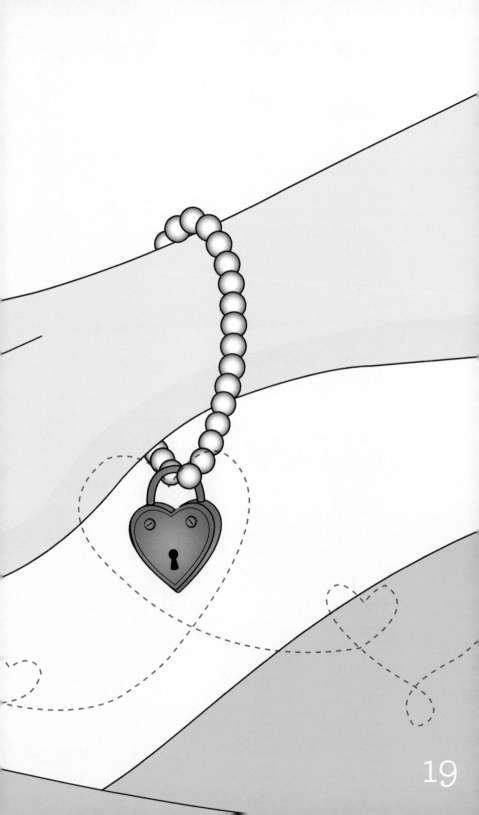

Your
Inner Goddess
won't be doing
cartwheels, axels,
twirls or flips.

No arabesques or
pole-vaults or
biting lower lips.

No samba, tango, merengue.
No cha-cha, karaoke.

Instead she'll sing
Twinkle Twinkle Little Star
and dance the Hokey Pokey.

23

Your Subconscious will
shake her head,
purse her lips,
fold her arms,
roll her eyes,
cringe, tut,
snort, sneer, scowl, stare,
gape, glare, gaze
at all the ways
you do it wrong.

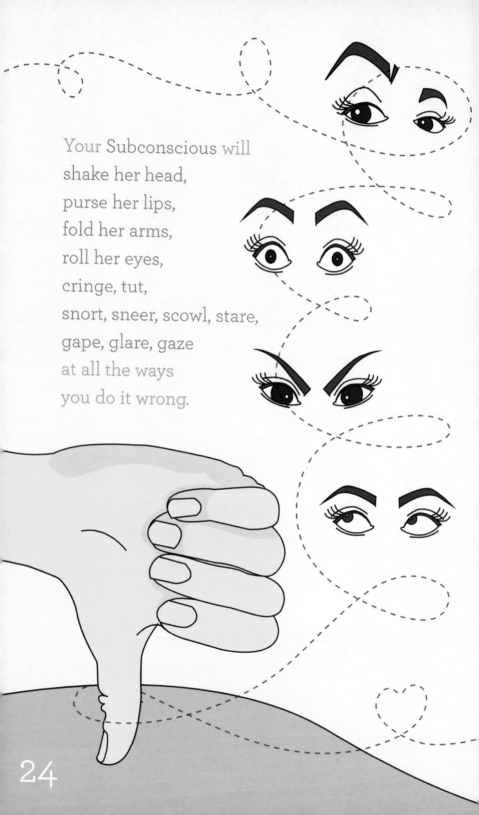

But your baby knows
no one but YOU
could do justice to this song.

You will sway and swing
your babe to sleep,
awake from dusk 'til dawn.

While your
Subconscious
stands by eyeing you,
her Edvard Munch face on.

You'll somehow slip from
Shades of Grey to
50 Shades of Pink.

Hey, don't judge.
You'll understand.
It happens faster
than you think.

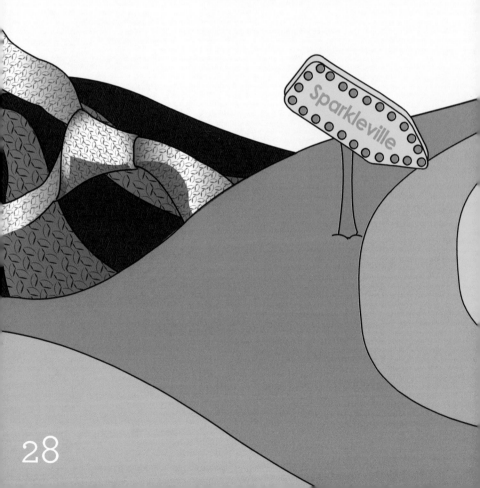

Pink bedding,
towels,
blankets.
Pink puzzles,
balls and bling.

Pink crayons, markers,
cookies, cupcakes,
sprinkles and frosting.

Pink dresses, shoes.
Pink socks.
Pink fairy wings
that flitter.
Pink rhinestones,
sparkles,
sequins,
glitter,
glitter,
glitter,
GLITTER!!!

33

34

Pink pants, tops,
panties, shorts.
Pink carpets,
drapes and walls.

Pink ribbons, hairbands,
tutus, bikes.
Pink movies, toys and dolls.

35

only 18 more years
'til college

FOR
SALE

36

Pink helmets, skates
and ski gear.
Pink boots and
pink raincoat.

Princesses, Barbies,
bubbles, face paint.
We need a bigger boat!

You will no longer be
all breath hitching
and palm twitching.

You'll be "where am I
supposed to house
ALL THIS PINK SHIT?"
bitching.

No smell of
fresh laundered linen
and expensive body wash.

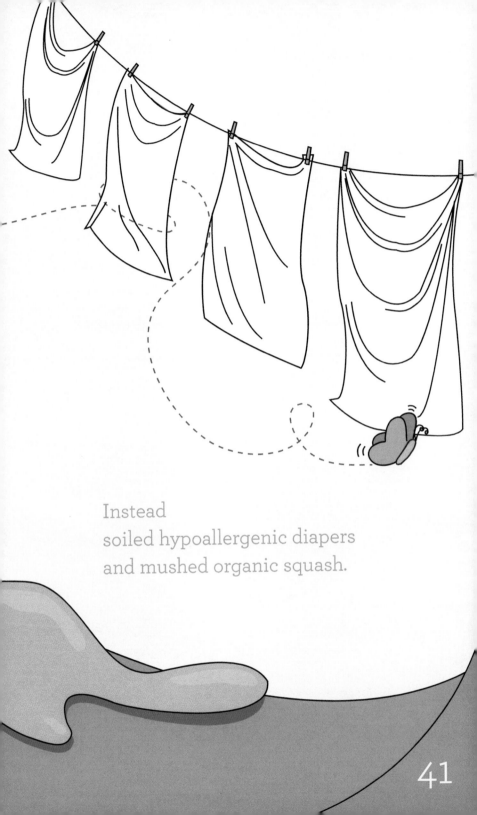

Instead
soiled hypoallergenic diapers
and mushed organic squash.

No Dad with pants
that hang from
his hips just in that way.

Just baby
with a load hanging
that can stay like that
all day.

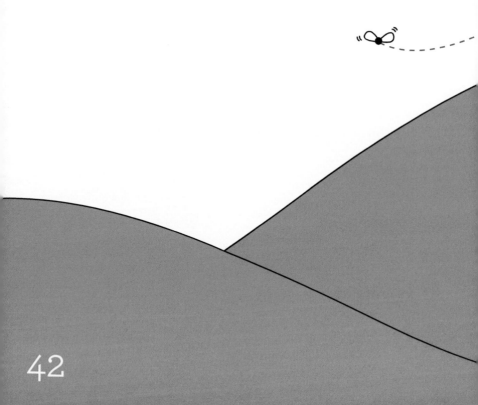

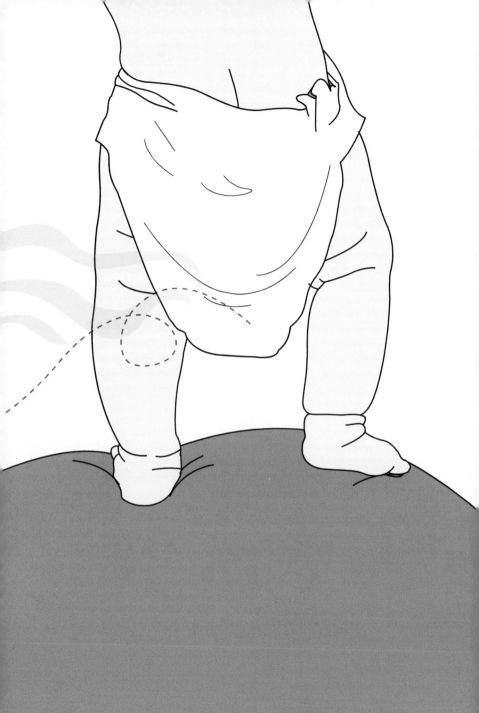

Your babe will be outfitted
to perfection,
a little doll
beautifully gowned.

While your own shirt
will be inside-out
and turned
the wrong way round.

Motherhood
may not end up
the way it was portrayed.

But who could explain
living with your heart
outside your body?
Fair point well made.

Will you have another?
Yes or no or maybe?

Baby's crying. Gotta run. See ya.
"Laters, Baby!"

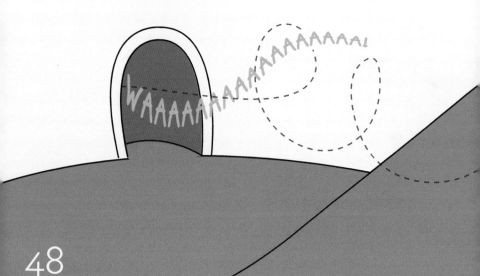

49

29174475R00030

Made in the USA
Charleston, SC
06 May 2014